UNFORGETTABLE
CATASTROPHES

TIME
FOR KIDS

D0834384

Tamara Leigh Hollingsworth

Consultants

Timothy Rasinski, Ph.D.
Kent State University

Lori Oczkus
Literacy Consultant

Based on writing from
TIME For Kids. *TIME For Kids* and the *TIME For Kids* logo are registered trademarks of TIME Inc. Used under license.

Publishing Credits

Dona Herweck Rice, *Editor-in-Chief*
Lee Aucoin, *Creative Director*
Jamey Acosta, *Senior Editor*
Heidi Fiedler, *Editor*
Lexa Hoang, *Designer*
Stephanie Reid, *Photo Editor*
Rane Anderson, *Contributing Author*
Rachelle Cracchiolo, *M.S.Ed., Publisher*

Image Credits: Cover, p.1 Getty Images; p.49 Alamy; pp.48–49 Adams County Historical Society; pp.26, 28 (left) AGE fotostock; pp.18–19 Associated Press; p.21 (bottom) FDR Presidential Library; pp.14–15, 20, 23 (bottom), 56–57, 57 (top) Getty Images; pp.52, 54, 54–55, 55 Library of Congress; p.29 (bottom) Lefranc David/ABACA/Newscom; p.47 AFP/Getty Images/Newscom; pp.30–31, p.26 akg-images/Newscom; pp.28–29 Paramount Home Media Distribution/Newscom; pp.38–39 EPA/Newscom; p.50 (bottom) Cezaro De Luca/ EPA/Newscom; p.41 Maschietto/MCT/Newscom; pp.36–37 Sean Gardner/Reuters/Newscom; p.36 AFP/Getty Images/Newscom; p.19 ZUMA Press/Newscom; pp.38, 52–53 NOAA; pp.46–47 (illustrations) Jim Kopp for TIME for Kids; p.44 RIA Novosti/Photo Researchers, Inc.; p.39 Photo Researchers, Inc.; p.7 US Air Force; pp.3, 34–35 U.S. Coast Guard; pp.20–21 Public Domain; p.53 (top) USDA; p.56 Lawrence Livermore National Security (CC-BY-SA); p.31 (bottom) National Archives; pp.17–18, 33 (top), 50–51 (illustrations) John Scahill; pp.32–33 (illustrations) Timothy J. Bradley; All other images from Shutterstock.

Teacher Created Materials

5301 Oceanus Drive
Huntington Beach, CA 92649-1030
http://www.tcmpub.com

ISBN 978-1-4333-4946-1

© 2013 Teacher Created Materials, Inc.

TABLE OF CONTENTS

DEADLY MISTAKES

Volcanoes. Earthquakes. Hurricanes. Tornadoes. Disasters come when we least expect them and turn our lives upside down. They can fall from the sky or rise up from the ground. These events are terrifying, but often we know when they are coming. We can prepare for them.

But some of the worst **catastrophes** are those caused by humans, and they usually come as a huge surprise. Sometimes, man-made disasters are **accidental**. They happen because of flaws in a design. They happen because a structure was poorly planned or built. Other times, people are aware of the power they are unleashing. These are **intentional** man-made disasters. And they can be the deadliest of all. They say the only real mistake is one you don't learn from. And there's plenty to learn from here.

THINK LINK

> What are some of the worst catastrophes in history?

> How can we prepare for these terrible events?

> How can we avoid repeating these mistakes in the future?

Making mistakes is part of being human. But sometimes, those mistakes can have big consequences. And often, the mistakes we make can be prevented.

Sometimes, a catastrophe is out of our control. Even when we are sure nothing will go wrong, something can still go wrong. But people try to be safe. And in most countries, there are laws that force workers to follow strict safety rules.

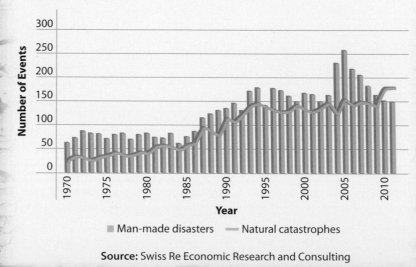

Running the Numbers

New technology and safety practices mean man-made disasters are currently on the decline. Because they can be deadly, man-made disasters may be featured heavily on the news. But these events are actually very rare.

Source: Swiss Re Economic Research and Consulting

QUICK FIX?

When *natural* disasters occur, the natural world may one day return to the way it was before the disaster. But with many *man-made* disasters, that's not the case. Sometimes, the damage done by humans is too great to be undone.

RECENT DISASTERS

In 2011, 325 catastrophic events occurred around the world. One hundred fifty of them were man-made. And of those 150 disasters, 5,703 lives were lost.

53.8%

7.7%

6.5%

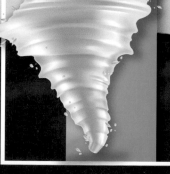

Natural Catastrophes   **Major Fires or Explosions**   **Aviation Disasters**

Look closely at these recent disasters. Which ones do you think could have been prevented? The answer may not be clear. An event such as a fire may be caused by a bolt of lighting. That would be difficult to prevent. But a fire could also be caused by someone dropping a match in a forest. The real catastrophe is being careless.

12%

20%

Maritime Disasters

Other

IN THE AIR

Curiosity fueled the quest to put humans in the air. For hundreds of years, **engineers** studied how animals fly. There were many failures. But finally, they created machines that sent humans soaring through the sky just like the birds.

Airplanes are complicated. And they do amazing things. It's very rare, but sometimes, something goes wrong. Still, flying is actually one of the safest ways to travel. Today, there are fewer accidents than ever before.

SAFE WITH SULLY

Pilot Chelsey B. "Sully" Sullenberger was able to guide his plane full of passengers to safety in a water landing known as the "Miracle on the Hudson."

TIME TRAVEL

Flying is a relatively new way to travel. A few hundred years ago, people rarely traveled long distances to visit someone. Very wealthy people could travel in carriages. But these days, travel has become something most people can do.

Hindenburg

Before airplanes, people traveled in **airships**. Just as the word hints, this type of flying machine looked like a ship on the inside. Unlike the airplanes used today, people could walk around in them or sit at tables.

The *Hindenburg* was a famous airship. It was made to fly people between the United States and Europe. It required huge amounts of fuel and used **flammable** gases to fly. In May 1937, disaster struck as the airship exploded as it tried to land.

AIRSHIP FLIGHT

The *Hindenburg's* frame was made of an aluminum alloy, a mixture of light and strong metals. It was covered with fabric and coated in a metallic substance. This substance was used to protect the gas from the sun's **radiation**.

Hydrogen was the first type of gas used to lift airships.

The company Goodyear flies airships to remind people to buy its products.

In 1937, spectators watched from the ground as flames engulfed the *Hindenburg*. It looked like a fireball dropping from the sky. Thirty-six people died on board, but another 64 survived.

What went wrong? The cause of this air disaster is a matter of debate. No one knows for sure. Some thought the back flaps of the airship opened and leaked gas. Some thought the airship was **sabotaged**. Others thought lightning struck the airship, setting it aflame, but most believe a mechanical problem was to blame. Somehow, fuel, sparks from the engine, and leaking gases combined and ignited. Because the gases flowed throughout the airship, the whole *Hindenburg* went up in flames. After the *Hindenburg* disaster, no airships of this kind were built again until after the late 1990s. When technology improved, people were able to fly safely and securely. Changes to the way the airships use flammable gases have made them much safer.

The *Hindenburg* carried mail between Europe and North America.

Airships Today

It's not common, but people can still fly in airships today. Most airships are used for special events and sightseeing trips.

INSIDE AN AIRSHIP

Airships were like cruise ships that could fly. There weren't long rows of seats or seatbelts. There were dining rooms and large libraries for reading. Take a tour of the *Hindenburg* to see what all the excitement was about.

kitchen

smoking lounge

There was a smoking room on board. The room was protected by a double-door air lock so hydrogen couldn't leak in. And only one electric lighter was allowed in the room at all times.

reading room

cabin

passenger cabins

Deck A included a dining room, a lounge, a writing room, 25 large cabins for passengers, and walkways for taking in the view.

reading room

dining room

crew dining

crew quarters

Challenger

Much was learned from the *Hindenburg* disaster, but in 1986, there was another terrible fire in the sky. On January 28th, the *Challenger* space shuttle exploded. It was just a minute into its flight. Across the country, people watched as the shuttle flew into pieces. All seven **astronauts** aboard were killed in the flames.

Like the *Hindenburg*, flammable gases came in contact with a fire. It ignited the whole structure. And as with the great airship disaster, people watched and learned. Later, changes were made to the design and testing of space shuttles.

REMARKABLE MEMORIES

Where were you when the Challenger exploded? That's a great question to ask your parents. When something like this happens, it impacts the entire nation, sometimes even the whole world. People remember where they were when they first heard the news. Years later, they'll still remember.

A Country Mourns

After the explosion, President Ronald Reagan gave a speech. He spoke about his sadness and the honor the astronauts deserved. A few days later, a memorial was held for the astronauts, including the first teacher sent into space. Over 10,000 people attended the funeral.

President Ronald Reagan

Hiroshima and Nagasaki

Not all man-made disasters are accidents. There have been moments in history when the damage was done intentionally. In August 1945, during the war, the United States dropped two **atomic bombs** from the sky.

It's well known that bombs are deadly, but war is deadly, too. World War II had already brought death and **devastation** to hundreds of thousands of people. To save lives in the long run, the United States took drastic measures. The country wanted to bring about an end to the war. And the United States thought the atomic bombs would end it.

PEARL HARBOR

The United States didn't enter World War II right away. On December 7, 1941, Japanese planes attacked the military base in Pearl Harbor, Hawaii. Over 2,300 Americans were killed.

Pearl Harbor from above

D-DAY

A day after the bombing of Pearl Harbor, President Franklin D. Roosevelt gave a speech. He wanted to convince the public to declare war on Japan. Roosevelt said that December 7th, 1941, was "a date that will live in infamy." Today, this date is still famous.

Both the instant and the lasting effects of the atomic bombs were horrific. The first bomb was aimed at the city of Hiroshima. It killed over 70,000 people. Then, a huge fireball rolled out where the bomb landed. It destroyed everything within four miles. Many were scared another bomb would fall. Some fled to the nearby city of Nagasaki. But three days later, the United States dropped a bomb there, too. It killed over 35,000 people.

Nuclear bombs are deadly. And the effects can last for years. In addition to killing so many people, atomic bombs also poison the water, the air, and the land. For many years after the attack, people suffered and died. The radiation from the bomb caused cancer and other illnesses. Today, people around the world are working to promote peace. They want to ensure these bombs are never used again.

JAPAN

Tokyo

Hiroshima

Nagasaki

MUSHROOM CLOUD

Nuclear bombs explode in a certain way. Unlike other types of bombs, nuclear bombs create a mushroom-shaped cloud that swells high into the air.

Years later, a blind man still suffers the effects of the bomb.

LONG-TERM ILLNESSES

The deaths from the atomic bombs did not stop when the fire went out or the war was over. Years after the bomb, people became blind or developed cancer in their eyes. Between 1950 and 1960, large numbers of people in Japan developed leukemia, a cancer of the blood or bones. And still today, cancer rates are higher than normal in Japan.

STOP AND BREATHE

The best way to prevent future disasters is to be prepared. Modern engineers have learned from past mistakes by building better bridges, ships, and planes. You can also prepare for disaster by taking certain steps to ensure your safety. Talk with your family about the tips below.

 Store canned goods so you will have food to eat if you lose electricity and cannot cook.

 Store enough water for three days. Each person in your family should have a gallon of water per day.

 Move your bed away from windows or mirrors to make your room safer during an earthquake.

 Keep your heaviest items on the lowest shelves to avoid damage or injury.

 Install smoke detectors and a fire extinguisher in your house.

 Discuss where the emergency items are located.

 Decide on a safe place where your family can meet if you get separated during a catastrophe.

 Create an emergency kit that contains a flashlight, walking shoes, a whistle, local maps, water, food, sleeping bags, money, and any medications you might need during a disaster.

STOP! THINK...

- Are there other things you can do to prepare for a catastrophe?

- What are some catastrophes you have read about in this book that could have been prevented and/or better prepared for?

- If you had three things you could bring in your emergency kit, what would they be?

EMERGENCY PREPARA
CHECKLIS

Section 1: Emergency Survival Items:

☐ Water Containers
☐ First Aid Kit
☐ Torch
☐ Battery Operated
☐ Batteries
☐ Tinned F
☐ Can

AT SEA

Humans have traveled across Earth's bodies of water for thousands of years. But like any creature, we have our limits. The sea is a dangerous place. And sometimes, it's humans that make it dangerous. Catastrophes at sea are often called **maritime disasters**. And many are unforgettable.

NAVIGATION

In 1418, Prince Henry of Portugal opened the first navigation school. It taught students to use the stars to pinpoint their location, to make maps, and to identify marine life. Without this knowledge, ships would become lost at sea. And that would be disastrous.

Although a ship sinks about once a week, most shipwrecks are too small to be widely reported.

TITANIC

Before people could travel by plane, they traveled between Europe and the United States on huge ships. One of the most famous ships to sail the seas was the *Titanic*. It was built using the most up-to-date science and technology. It was **heralded** as unsinkable. In April 1912, the *Titanic* left England for its first voyage. There were about 2,200 people on board, but there were only enough lifeboats for half that number. When the ship hit an iceberg four days later, the unsinkable ship sank.

The Titanic sank in less than three hours.

HIGH FLYING

The *Titanic* had luxuries never before seen on any ship, including a swimming pool, an indoor gym, and places on board to play sports. It also had a reading and writing room for people to sit by the fire and a dining room reserved for the wealthiest passengers.

At 11:40 P.M., in the **frigid** Atlantic Ocean, the *Titanic* hit an iceberg. The impact only lasted about 10 seconds, but it tore open the ship. The ship began to fill with water. The lights stayed on, and no one knew how fatal the damage was. People stayed inside their rooms, unafraid. But below deck was a disaster zone. When the **evacuation** began, many of the lifeboats weren't full. But by 2:20 A.M., the whole ship was under water. Those on lifeboats waited. It took two hours before help arrived. Accidents like this are very rare, but the memory of the *Titanic* pushes all sailors to be as safe as possible.

CARPATHIA

The *Carpathia* was 58 miles away from the *Titanic* when it heard the *Titanic's* call for help over the radio. The *Carpathia* sailed as fast as it could and rescued those who were still alive. The captain and crew received medals of honor for their rescue.

CANCELED DRILL

As the boat sank, some passengers stayed in their rooms. They might not have known what to do. In fact, the ship's captain had canceled the lifeboat safety drill earlier that day. More people may have survived if they had known what to do in an emergency.

IN SHIP SHAPE

After the *Titanic* sank, safety rules were developed to ensure ships would always carry enough lifeboats to hold everyone on board. Ships began sailing farther away from icebergs as well.

DIG DEEPER!

CLASS SYSTEM

The *Titanic* was like a floating city, home to a wide variety of people. Some were rich. Some were poor. When it came time to escape the sinking ship, the wealthiest people were allowed onto lifeboats. The poorest people were not allowed on deck until some of the wealthier people were safe.

THIRD CLASS CABIN

The smallest rooms were used by families moving from Europe to the United States. Many had sold all their belongings to buy their tickets. Families paid $32 to $50 for their third-class tickets. That's about $740 to $1,100 today.

The largest cabins were reserved for the wealthiest people. The first class rooms were about 10 by 12 feet. A few had telephones. Some included private dining and kitchen areas. Fares ranged from $75 to $325.

FIRST CLASS CABIN

SECOND CLASS CABIN

Teachers, farmers, and businessmen stayed in second class. These people had worked to achieve their money and success. Fares ranged from $17 to $99.

BP Oil Spill

Oil is used for everything from heating our homes to fueling our cars. We search high and low for this precious liquid. And we go to extreme lengths to draw it from the Earth.

British **Petroleum** (BP) is a large company that drills for oil in the ocean floor. In April 2010, the Deepwater Horizon **oil rig** exploded. The explosion killed 11 people and blew a hole in a pipe deep under the water.

OIL RIGS

Offshore oil rigs are raised platforms built over the water. In the center, a large drill digs for oil. A hose brings it to the surface. Most oil rigs have about a hundred workers on them at a time. Over water and far from land, it's hard to rescue people when there is trouble on an oil rig.

Exxon Valdez Oil Spill

In 1989, a huge barge carrying over 50 million gallons of oil from Alaska hit a reef. Oil gushed into the water off the Alaskan coast. The spill happened in a remote area, so cleanup and rescue took time. The effects on wildlife were **tragic**.

Once the underground pipe burst, oil poured into the Gulf of Mexico. No one could dive deep enough to repair it. BP tried using machines to stop the oil from flowing, but that didn't work.

From April to July, oil continued to spill. Birds, fish, and sea animals were harmed. They were covered in oil and couldn't breathe or clean themselves. The spilled oil made 320 miles of coastline unusable. This terrible disaster left 4,200 square miles **contaminated**. And the 80 miles that surrounded the Deepwater Horizon was declared a **dead zone**. Today, people are working together to restore life to the area. Others are finding ways to prevent future spills.

an underwater view of oil gushing from the oil rig

TRY, TRY, AGAIN...

BP tried many things to stop the oil from spilling. They tried machines to cap the place where the oil was leaking. They put huge pieces of metal down into the ground to try to plug the leak. They even shot golf balls into the hole. Each day, people could watch live video of BP trying to stop the leak. Finally, in July, a 40-ton sealing cap stopped the spill.

A HARD SELL

The fishing industry was hit hard. Because of the oil in the water, there were no fish to sell. With no fish to buy, the restaurants in the area couldn't sell food. The entire coastal economy was devastated by the spill.

ONE YEAR LATER

The immediate effects of the BP oil spill were easy to spot: dark, murky, oily water, and animals such as fish, birds, turtles, and seals covered in thick, black oil. But what about one year after the disaster? Did the ocean heal from this horrendous disaster? Did the Gulf of Mexico return to its once sparkling blue hue? And what happened to the 4.4 million barrels of oil that spilled into the ocean?

A researcher checks water samples for natural gas and oil.

Oil degrading marine bacteria helped break down oil from the spill.

MISSING IN ACTION

One year after the BP oil spill, millions of barrels of oil were still missing in the ocean. That's enough oil to power the whole world for eight minutes! So where did it go? Bacteria had digested most of the oil. Only six months had passed when scientists studied the spill area and said the water was returning to normal. This time, the ocean made a natural recovery.

Great Pacific Garbage Patch

The Great Pacific Garbage Patch is a swirling mass of trash. It's in the northern part of the Pacific Ocean. How did it get there? Rainwater flushed garbage down rivers until it reached the ocean. And somehow, it kept ending up in the same place. Much of it is formed by tiny pieces of plastic. Since plastic isn't **biodegradable**, it stays put. Most of the trash is too small to be seen with the human eye. But it has a big impact on the sea. The plastic leaks harmful chemicals into the water. And this man-made waste endangers wildlife. Fortunately, this is a catastrophe that can easily be prevented. Recycling efforts are making our waters cleaner and safer.

BIODEGRADING

Food and paper waste breaks down naturally. This is biodegradable waste. It doesn't make plants or animals sick. Non-biodegradable things do. As plastic degrades, it breaks down into chemicals that harm water, soil, plants, and animals.

GARBAGE AT SEA

The Great Pacific Garbage Patch is created by plastic debris and other trash from around the world that is brought together by ocean currents, shown as red arrows below.

RUSSIA

Oyashio
Bering

CANADA

Alaska

North Pacific

UNITED STATES

JAPAN

Kuroshio

California

MEXICO

The Great Pacific Garbage Patch resides within this slow-moving zone that allows floating debris to build up.

The patch's precise size is not known, but some scientists estimate it to be twice the size of Texas.

Hawaiian Islands

North Equatorial

Equatorial Countercurrent

South Equatorial

Source: National Oceanic and Atmospheric Association

CURRENT ISSUES

The currents in the major oceans all move in a circular pattern. The Great Pacific Garbage Patch is not the only one of its kind. The currents in the Atlantic Ocean move trash to a central spot as well. The mass of trash in the Pacific Ocean is much larger, however.

ON THE GROUND

Each day, people interact with the dirt, soil, and land. They harvest food and energy to **sustain** themselves and their communities. The land benefits people in many ways. It provides food and water to eat and drink, wood to burn and build with, and coal and oil to help machines run. The Earth is precious to us, but this precious **commodity** can become tainted or polluted. It can collapse, destroying itself and the people nearby. It can even become **barren**, dried up, and unable to grow plants. If we destroy the very land we live on, where will we live? Where will we farm? And what will we eat?

SUSTAINABLE FARMING

Farming requires a lot of water and energy. **Sustainable farming** happens when farms grow products that can be grown again easily and naturally. This type of farming is gentle on the Earth and leaves less room for disasters.

Large vehicles are used for a wide variety of tasks and require large amounts of fuel.

Wood is burned to create heat and is used as fuel.

Fossil Fuels

Fuel is needed to make everyday things such as dishwashers and cars run. But the fuel must come from somewhere. The fuel we use has been stored underground for thousands of years. When Earth is damaged, our resources are also at risk.

Chernobyl

Nuclear radiation is used in many places to power homes and factories. Nuclear power plants are monitored to ensure they do not release dangerous radiation. If there is trouble, the plants are designed to shut down until things are safe. But, sometimes, something can go wrong. The events at Chernobyl, a nuclear power plant in Russia, are an example of a nuclear disaster.

On April 26, 1986, there was an explosion at the power plant. Huge amounts of radiation were released. It was much stronger than the radiation released from an atomic bomb. A poisonous cloud of nuclear gas filled the air. It traveled across Russia. It spread as far away as Finland. Plant life around the power plant died. Strange **mutations** were later found in both people and animals. But the long-term effects of the radiation are still unknown.

children playing near a nuclear plant

Millions of people still live in the contaminated area around the plant.

WHY NUCLEAR ENERGY?

Nuclear energy may be dangerous, but many people believe it's the energy of the future. Coal and oil have a hazardous effect on the environment. Nuclear power causes less pollution and may keep our planet cleaner.

TOTAL MELTDOWN

Chernobyl wasn't the last nuclear accident the world would see. A little more than 20 years later, Japan would endure its own nuclear power-plant disaster. On March 11, 2011, a magnitude 9.0 earthquake ripped through Japan's northeastern coast. The quake triggered a tsunami with waves as high as a three-story building. The quake and tsunami disabled the Fukushima power plant's cooling system. Helicopters and crews dumped seawater into the reactors to prevent overheating. Despite these efforts, the plant suffered several explosions and fires, causing some radiation to escape. Residents were evacuated to prevent exposure to dangerous radiation.

HOW A TSUNAMI FORMS

In a tsunami, long ocean waves gather strength and height, and spill onto land. The powerful waves are produced by a quake or volcanic eruption under the sea. The March 11 tsunami set off warnings as far away as the West Coast of the United States.

1

THE COLLISION
Large plates in the Earth's crust shift, releasing lots of energy. Vast volumes of water are displaced, causing a tsunami.

NORTH AMERICAN PLATE

PACIFIC PLATE

Cameras captured these images of the plant exploding from afar.

2

THE TSUNAMI
In the sea, the waves start out long and low. The tsunami gains power and height as it speeds toward land.

NORTH AMERICAN PLATE

PACIFIC PLATE

West Virginia Coal Mine

Coal is another source of power people use. But **mining** coal is dirty and risky work. To find the coal, miners set off dangerous explosions. They travel underground through tight tunnels. It is rare, but every miner knows the tunnels may collapse with little warning.

In 1907, in the town of Monongah, West Virginia, the ground began to shake violently. Deep below, two explosions rocked the local coal mine. The air was filled with flammable gases. The explosion set the air on fire. Four men near the surface escaped. One more man was later pulled from the **rubble**. The rest of the 362 men and young boys underground died. It left close to 1,000 families without fathers, brothers, and sons.

RESCUING THE RESCUERS

Rescuing trapped miners is dangerous. The rescue workers risk their lives and may become trapped, too.

entrance to a mine

SAFETY FIRST

Miners know the work they do is risky. They put safety first and try to minimize the risks whenever possible. New technology and safety laws are making their job safer than before.

DIG DEEPER!

A HAPPY ENDING

Sometimes, even a catastrophe can have a happy ending. In 2010, 33 Chilean miners were trapped more than 2,000 feet underground in a mining disaster that could have turned deadly. Instead, it became a story that inspired the world.

Experts estimated it would take three to four months to drill a spiral tunnel large enough to carry the miners to the surface. They thought rushing the process could result in another dangerous collapse. Rescuers decided not to tell the men.

Over two months later, all 33 miners were rescued alive.

In the beginning, each miner ate two teaspoons of tuna and one biscuit every two days. Later, rescuers delivered food, water, medicine, and oxygen through a six-inch tunnel.

The miners set up their living area as best they could. They dug for water and assigned an area to be used as a bathroom. The only light was from the miners' helmets.

To keep up their spirits, the men played games, read letters from loved ones, and exercised. One miner ran nearly six miles a day through the mine tunnels.

The Dust Bowl

Explosives and chemicals aren't the only man-made disasters that can kill. Sometimes, people fail to take care of the land. When that happens, the land can no longer take care of them. In order to keep farmlands healthy, farmers must **rotate** crops. They must leave some fields **fallow**, or unplanted. This allows the land to remain healthy and able to grow plants. For years, American farmers in the Midwest did not maintain their farmlands. So when a severe drought hit in the early 1930s, the ground dried up. Huge, dark clouds of dust moved across the plains in the middle of the United States. This time of scarcity became known as the Dust Bowl.

CROP SAFETY

In order to keep crops growing and farmlands healthy, farmers must use certain techniques. But because there was such high demand for farm products, farmers skipped some important steps. The Dust Bowl would have been easier if farmers had been able to take better care of the land.

BLACK SUNDAY

One of the most terrifying scenes from the Dust Bowl was Black Sunday. On that Sunday, 60-mile-per-hour winds gathered thousands of pounds of dust into huge moving clouds. These clouds of dust were so thick they covered the light from the sun.

During the drought, powerful winds swept across the dry soil. The wind picked up the top layers of dust from off the ground. This created moving walls of dust. Close to a million acres of land in Oklahoma, Texas, Kansas, Colorado, and New Mexico are still unusable today.

Sadly, the Dust Bowl took place during the **Great Depression**. When farmers were forced to leave their farms, there were few jobs waiting for them. Nearly 2.5 million farmers were homeless and without a way to make money.

OKIES

One famous term coined during the Dust Bowl was Okie. This was the name given to a person who had left Oklahoma in search of new opportunities. Many of those who left the plains traveled west to places like California.

Families carried all their belongings with them as they moved west to try to escape the Dust Bowl.

REMEMBERING

The Grapes of Wrath is a novel by John Steinbeck. It tells the story of an Oklahoma family hurt by the Dust Bowl. Like many people of the time, the family must live and work in poor conditions. They try to improve their lives by moving to California. The novel is considered an American classic because it so clearly and truthfully describes the people and the time.

Families that couldn't afford houses were forced to live in tents and simple wood shelters.

LEARNING FROM OUR MISTAKES

Each day, the world's greatest engineers and scientists are working to improve our lives. That may mean creating better farming tools, finding new ways to dig up more oil, or building a faster flying machine. New technology may bring new risks. But it also makes our lives safer and healthier.

People read old newspapers to learn about the *Hindenburg* and the *Challenger*. There are museums to honor those who died in West Virginia, Hiroshima, and Nagasaki. And movies and novels tell the story of the Dust Bowl and *Titanic*. Humanity's desire to understand and learn from its mistakes can be seen everywhere. Together, we remember so we can do better.

A factory worker performs safety checks at a power plant.

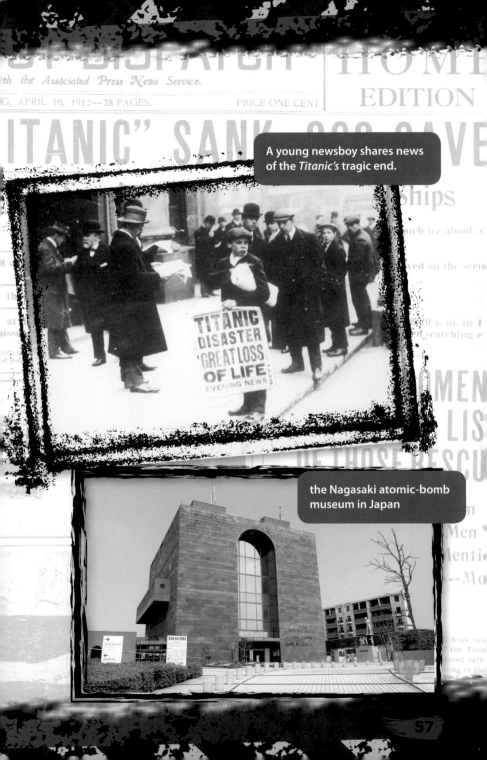

A young newsboy shares news of the *Titanic's* tragic end.

the Nagasaki atomic-bomb museum in Japan

GLOSSARY

accidental—something that happens but is not planned

airships—ships filled with a gas that is lighter than air (for example, hydrogen) and are able to float and steer in the sky

astronauts—people who travel into space

atomic bombs—bombs that get power from a specific kind of nuclear energy

barren—unable to reproduce

biodegradable—able to naturally break down into small pieces that can be used again

catastrophes—sudden, widespread disasters

commodity—something of use, advantage, or value, such as crops

contaminated—to be tainted, dirty, or unsanitary

dead zone—an area in a body of water with low oxygen levels that is unable to support life

devastation—complete ruin

engineers—people who use math and science to build things

evacuation—removing people from a place of danger

fallow—a piece of land left unseeded for a season

flammable—easily lit on fire

frigid—extremely cold

Great Depression—the economic crisis that began with the stock market crash in 1929 and continued through most of the 1930s

heralded—announced and publicized

intentional—something that happens that is planned

maritime disasters—catastrophes that deal with ships and the sea

mining—obtaining resources from a pit or excavation in the surface of the Earth

mutations—changes in the makeup of something so it results in something different

nuclear—of or relating to the atomic nucleus

oil rig—a structure above an oil well on land or in the sea that has special equipment attached to it for drilling and removing oil from the ground

petroleum—a kind of oil that comes from underground and is the source for gasoline and other products

radiation—the process in which waves or pieces of energy are put out

rotate—to select a series of different crops that use and benefit the soil in different ways.

rubble—pieces of things that have been broken

sabotaged—deliberately damaged or destroyed

sustain—to keep up or to keep going

sustainable farming—the practice of farming to grow products that can be easily and naturally grown again

tragic—extremely sad

INDEX

BIBLIOGRAPHY

Bredeson, Carmen. *The Challenger Disaster: Tragic Space Flight (American Disasters).* **Enslow Pub Inc., 1999.**

Discover the events surrounding the tragic shuttle explosion. You'll also learn about the seven crew members of the *Challenger*, including Christa McAuliffe, who would have been the first teacher in space.

Brewster, Hugh. *Inside the Titanic (A Giant Cutaway Book).* **Little, Brown and Company, 1997.**

Join two real-life young passengers aboard the *Titanic* to experience their journey before the ship sank, their rescue, and their lives after the tragic event. Fold-out pages reveal amazing cutaway floor plans of the ship.

Platt, Richard and Richard Bonson. *Disaster! Catastrophes That Shook the World.* **DK Children, 1997.**

Go behind the scenes of the most destructive catastrophes in history, including natural disasters, accidents, and plagues. Full-color cross-sectional artwork and detailed text bring these events to life.

Tarshis, Lauren. *I Survived the San Francisco Earthquake, 1906.* **Scholastic, 2012.**

The *I Survived* books are not based on real people, but all the historical events are true. In this exciting book, you can experience the terrifying 1906 San Francisco earthquake through the eyes of Leo, a 10-year-old newsboy.

MORE TO EXPLORE

Airships: *The Hindenburg* and other Zeppelins
http://www.airships.net/

Explore the history of airships such as the *Hindenburg*. Learn about airship technology and the amazing people who made these ships possible. Tons of photos and facts help you imagine what it was like aboard these massive floating giants.

National Geographic Kids: Green Scene
http://kidsblogs.nationalgeographic.com/greenscene/gulf-oil-spill.html

Read about the 2010 oil spill in the Gulf of Mexico. Find out more about its aftermath, and view images and videos of the resulting destruction to plant and animal life as well as the environment.

RMS Titanic, Inc.
http://www.rmstitanic.net/

Discover photos of artifacts and videos of the underwater wreckage from the *Titanic*. Go to the Learning Center to read more about facts, myths, and more. Click on Exhibitions to find out which museums currently have a *Titanic* collection.

Social Studies for Kids: Pearl Harbor Attack
http://www.socialstudiesforkids.com/subjects/pearlharbor.htm

Check out different links to sites about the Japanese attack on Hawaii during World War II. Explore interactive maps, listen to eyewitness accounts, follow event time lines, and more.

ABOUT THE AUTHOR

Tamara Leigh Hollingsworth was born and raised in Cupertino, California. She attended Hollins University, an all-women's college, in Roanoke, Virginia, where she earned a degree in English. While in college, she spent time traveling through Europe. Since then, she has been a high school English teacher who avoids disasters in and out of the classroom. She currently lives in Atlanta, Georgia. When she's not working with her beloved students, Tamara loves to spend time with her husband, her daughter, her books, and her iPod.